# Finger Plays

and

# How to Use Them

Edited by Tessa Colina
Illustrated by June K. Deist

# CONTENTS

# CONTENTS *(Continued)*

## Special Days

## Animals and Birds

## Fall and Winter

## Miscellaneous

# HOW TO USE FINGER PLAYS

Mary's class of four-year-olds watched her intently as she placed her hands to form a rabbit's ears, and then made the rabbit go into a hole by simply putting her right fist through the circle of her left arm. Their faces beamed. "Now let me see if you can do it," she said. And eight pairs of chubby hands began to imitate the motions as the teacher went through the finger play again. It took longer for some of the children than for others. And Mary had to stop occasionally and help an especially clumsy one, but when they had completed the finger play, the children all chorused, "Let's do it again!"

Perhaps you think that Mary was wasting her time and the children's time. Perhaps you think she should have been teaching them instead of playing with them. But the fact is, children learn more by doing than they do by seeing! And we are all acquainted with the value of visual aids.

Dramatic play is being used more and more in all phases of modern education. It is therefore only fitting to use this method in the Sunday school. In the precious formative years of the child's life every successful method should be used to impress upon him the truths of God's Word that he might be rightly prepared for life.

Many of us have failed to see that learning need not be drudgery. It can and should be fun. When it is, children will approach learning with more eagerness. And the truths learned will never be forgotten.

Finger plays were one of the earliest "doing" methods, and still remain one of the most popular, especially for teaching preschool children. However, Primary children like them, too. With their greater memory retention, they will soon learn them and can do them without the help of the teacher. The longer ones are better for them.

Finger plays can serve several helpful teaching purposes. Perhaps the first and most widely used is to help impress a story or thought previously taught. If the teacher has a story about God's world and follows with a finger play about a robin's nest or five baby squirrels, the story will be more deeply impressed in the child's mind.

Another fine use is for introducing a story. At the same time the finger play relaxes tired muscles and prepares the children physically for the story to come. Sometimes they may be used simply as an outlet for stored-up activity. They quiet a group of restless children who might not otherwise settle down for a story or worship period and that precious time would be wasted.

Children have rhythm. They seem to be born with it. Finger plays are a means by which they may be taught through a natural medium.

Finger plays stimulate the imagination. And children with their vivid imaginations will find joy in learning by such a method.

Finger plays help to train the memory of the child. For this reason they serve a double purpose.

Children are imitators, and imitation is the approach to learning the finger play employs. Watch Billy as he crosses his legs when he sees an adult do so, or repeats words and phrases immediately upon hearing them. You can readily see then, how important finger plays are in the development and training of the child.

The teacher who uses finger plays should know how to use them. She should use much expression not only in her voice but also in her hands and face. She should pronounce her words carefully in a low modulated voice.

Although the teacher should have a number of finger plays ready for use, she should not try to teach too many in a short time. Learning comes by repetition. Even though some should be used when there is a desire to teach a certain truth, the teacher should not ignore the children's favorites. When they say, "Let's do that one about the church," the teacher should oblige if time permits.

The teacher should never use a finger play until she has fully committed it to memory and knows the motions well. When she stumbles and fumbles, the children will be confused and their appreciation will be lessened.

Finger plays may be elaborated to take in fuller body movements with the children standing and even moving about. They may be set to music—simple tunes—if the teacher so desires. The teacher can use her imagination to improvise in many of the poems. She should not feel that she has to be a "slave" to a book, but she can use the poems merely as ideas to provide her own finger plays.

As the children, especially the older ones, learn the finger plays, they may be permitted to do the motions and say them individually, or lead the group activity. This often encourages the children to make greater effort to learn them.

Finger plays may be used in the Sunday school, the vacation Bible school, the nursery, the kindergarten, and the home. They may be used at any time the teacher desires. The alert teacher will use them wisely. She will use them skillfully. Her reward will be an enthusiastic group of youngsters who like to learn because learning is so much fun.

The finger plays in this book have been classified and graded. We have included not only many new ones, but several old favorites of both teachers and pupils through the years. At the top of each poem, the name of the age group or groups for which the finger play is best suited has been inserted. The finger plays have also been classified under several heads, so that it will be easy to find a suitable one.

# FINGER FUN

Ten fingers are a lot of fun!
    (Hold up fingers of both hands.)
They fold for prayer when day is done.
    (Fold hands and bow head.)
They help with tasks all through the day.
    (Have children take turns suggesting tasks to imitate here.)
With them I count my turn at play.
    (Count on fingers of one hand.)
I keep them busy as can be:
They lace my shoes and button me.
    (Stoop to lace shoes, then button imaginary buttons on clothes.)
They hold my fork so I can eat.
    (Go through motions of eating.)
They comb my hair so smooth and neat.
    (Go through motions of combing hair.)
They dance on the piano keys,
    (Play on imaginary piano.)
And do a hundred things that please.
    (Clap hands once in delight.)
                                    —*Thea Cannon.*

# Spring and Summer

# SPRING SHOWERS

The flower holds up its little cup;
> (Form cup with two hands.)

The tree holds out its leaves.
> (Hold out hands for leaves.)

That's the way the growing things
> (Repeat cup and leaf motions for this and next line.)

Have of saying, "please."

So when they're thirsty God sends down
> (For this and next line make rain motions with fingers.)

Many drops of rain;

And we can watch them patter pit
> (For this and the next line, cup chin in hands as if watching through window.)

Against our window pane.

—*Thea Cannon.*

11

# THE WAKING FLOWERS

*Beginners or Primary*

All the little flowers
Planted in a row,
In their beds are sleeping
(Children bow heads and close eyes.)
Till it's time to grow.

Wake, oh, little flowers,
(Children lift their heads, open eyes, and rise from seats.)
For the spring is here,
And the dainty blossoms
Bloom for children dear.

All the flowers are swaying,
(Children sway back and forth.)
Swaying in the breeze,
While they're nodding gaily
(Children nod.)
To the leafy trees.

—*Emma F. Bush*

# THE WIND CAME OUT FOR A FROLIC

*Primary*

The wind came out for a frolic one day.
He first swept the clouds all out of the way;
(Move right hand lightly upward.)
The weather vane turned wherever he blew,
(Right hand to turn like a weather vane.)
The trees bowed low, the leaves danced, too;
(Bend bodies low, then fingers dance.)
The wind blew a gale for the ships at sea,
(Hands together; thumbs up, moving like a boat.)
The wind tried to snatch my hat from me;
(Hands on head, as if to hold hat on.)
He really did get my Japanese kite,
And it sailed and sailed till it sailed out of sight;
(Move right hand slowly upward and backward.)
The wind whispered low, down my chimney flue,
And every word that he said was—"Oo-oo-oo!"
(Form chimney with hands and make the sound of "oo,"
first low, then high—down the chimney.)

—*Maud Burnham.*

# SAND CASTLE
### Beginners and Primary

I shovel sand in a pile so big.
> (Shoveling motions, then arms in wide circle for "so big.")

I pat it down, then dig, dig, dig
> (Pat imaginary pile, then digging motions with hand.)

A tunnel to the other side.
> (Keep digging and scooping dirt out of imaginary tunnel.)

I make some windows big and wide.
> (Poke holes with pointed index finger.)

In the top I poke a stick.
> (Use index finger—bring it straight down from head level to top of imaginary castle.)

That's the flag.  Now that was quick!
> (Point to flag and clap hands once.)

—*Thea Cannon.*

# SWIMMING
### Nursery and Beginners

I'm glad God gave us water.
> (Clap hands once.)

I jump and splash and—swish!
> (Splash with both hands, then put hands together in diving position for "swish" and following line.)

I dive down in the water,
And play that I'm a fish.
> (Keep hands together and wave arms like a swimming fish.)

—*Thea Cannon.*

13

# THE BABY ROBINS
*Primary*

A robin built a little nest,
> (Cup hands to form nest.)

And laid four tiny eggs of blue.
> (Use thumbs and index fingers to show little eggs.)

The mother kept the eggs real warm,
> (Place left hand over cupped nest of right hand.)

And God was watching, too.
> (Keep hands as above.)

Then crack and pop!  The blue eggs broke,
> (With "crack" take left hand off quickly, then make a snap with thumb and index finger.)

And snuggled in the robins' nest
> (Cup hands for nest.)

Were four small birds with mouths *so* big!
> (Hold up four fingers and then show big mouths with thumb and index fingers.)

And each had fuzz upon his chest!
> (Put hand on chest.)

*—Thea Cannon.*


# FIRST FLIGHT
*Beginners and Primary*

A baby bird fell from a tree,
> (Left hand held up is tree, and right fist is bird falling out.)

But God, of course, was there to see.
He kept the baby soft and warm,
> (Left hand laid over right fist.)

And shooed away all that could harm,
> (Left hand pushes away from bird.)

Until the mother bird came by
> (Hands held together at wrist and hands flap to fly.)

And showed her baby how to fly.
> (This time use thumbs for wings to show baby bird flying.)

*—Thea Cannon.*

# A RAIN STORY

*Beginners or Primary*

"Pitter, patter, pitter, patter,"
Hear the raindrops say,
But, if a sunbeam should peep out,
They'd make a rainbow gay.

"Rumble, rumble, rumble, rumble,"
Hear the thunder say,
But soon the clouds will all be gone,
And we'll go out to play.

(The "pitter, patter," of the raindrops is made by the fingers.
The fingers touch overhead and then separate so that arms
and hands indicate the wide, high arch of the rainbow.
Doubled-up fingers of the fist make the "rumble, rumble,"
as knuckles roll back and forth on table. Both hands overhead, finger tips touching, make clouds that separate and
go away.)

—*Louise M. Oglevee.*

# SPRING HAS COME

*Beginners*

"Wake up," said the little raindrops,
(Raindrops rise quickly from chairs.)
"Wake up," said the sunbeams, too.
(Sunbeams rise quickly.)
"Spring has come," sang a bird;
(Birds rise and flutter wings.)
Then the little flowers heard,
(Flowers rise slowly.)
So they all woke up and grew.
(Divide the children into four groups—raindrops, sunbeams,
birds and flowers.)

—*Lillien E. Landman.*

# IF I WERE A FLOWER

*Nursery and Beginners*

If I were a little flower,
Sleeping underneath the ground,
I'd raise my head and grow and grow,
And stretch my arms and grow and grow,
And nod my head and say,
"I love you, I love you, I love you."
(Do the motions the words suggest.)

—*Selected.*

# TEN LITTLE LEAF BUDS
*Primary*

Ten little leaf buds growing on a tree,
(Children have fingers outstretched for buds.)
Curled up as tightly as can be.
(Curl fingers up in tight fists.)
See them keeping snug and warm
During winter's cold and storm.
(Snuggle fists up under chin.)
Now along comes windy March
With his breath now soft, now harsh,
First he swings them roughly so,
(Swings fists back and forth.)
Then more gently to and fro.
(Now swings them tenderly.)
Till the raindrops from the skies
(Stretch arms high, bring them down to floor, tapping fingers
constantly to represent rain.)
Falling pitter-patter wise,
(Repeat previous movement.)
Open wide the leaf bud's eyes.
(With arms outstretched, open up fist and spread fingers
at the word "eyes.")

—*Luella Habenicht.*

# NIGHT AND MORNING
*Beginners and Primary*

This little boy is going to bed;
(First finger of the right hand in palm of left.)
Down on the pillow he lays his head;
(Thumb of left hand is pillow.)
Wraps himself in the covers tight—
(Fingers of left hand closed.)
This is the way he sleeps all night.

Morning comes, he opens his eyes;
Back with a toss the cover flies;
(Fingers of left hand open.)
Up he jumps, is dressed and away,
(Right index finger up and hopping away.)
Ready for frolic and play all day.

—*Unknown.*

# UMBRELLAS
## *Primary*

When flowers needed raindrops
>(Make raindrops come down with fingers.)

But people just got wet;
>(Continue raindrops.)

God thought of something very nice
>(Put hand to chin in thinking pose.)

So children wouldn't fret.
>(Point to self and other children.)

Now when rain is falling down
>(Raindrops again.)

We needn't pout and sigh,
>(Pout and sigh with words.)

For God gave us umbrellas
>(Place right hand over index finger of left hand to form umbrellas.)

To keep us snug and dry.
>(Place "umbrella" over head.)

—*Thea Cannon.*

17

# THE ROBIN'S NEST

*Beginners or Primary*

This is the nest that the robins made,
And these are the eggs so blue
That under the mother bird's soft breast
Hatched into these birdies two.

This is the way two hungry mouths
All day cried, "Tweet, tweet, tweet,"
While father and mother bird flew about
And found good food to eat.

This is the way the birdies perched
On the edge of the nest one day,
Till the mother bird taught them how to fly,
And all of them flew away.

> (The two cupped hands together make the nests, and the thumbs are first the eggs and then the little birds waving their wobbly heads. They perch on the edge of the nest, and when they all fly away, both hands are used.)

—*Louise M. Oglevee.*

# THE SLEEPY FLOWERS

*Primary*

This is the way the snow comes down
From the dark clouds falling,
With a blanket pure and white,
Cov'ring all the flowers from sight.
This is the way the snow comes down
From the dark clouds falling.

This is the way the rain comes down
From the dark clouds falling,
Tapping, tapping, as if to say:
"Wake up, flowers, so bright and gay."
This is the way the rain comes down
From the dark clouds falling.

> (The fingers imitate the whirling little snowflakes softly falling and making a smooth blanket over the flowers. The hands again, in the rain verse, make the clouds high in the air, but they fall with a "tapping, tapping," of the fingers on the table or the floor.

—*Louise M. Oglevee.*

## MY GARDEN
*Beginners and Primary*

I dig, dig, dig;
>(Make digging motions.)

I plant some seeds.
>(Place imaginary seeds in imaginary holes.)

I rake, rake, rake;
>(Make raking motions.)

I hoe some weeds.
>(Make hoeing motions.)

I wait and watch,
>(Place hands behind back, spread feet apart in waiting attitude.)

And soon right there
>(Point to garden.)

My garden sprouts—
>(Push fingers of right hand, as sprouts, through fingers of left hand, the ground.)

It's in God's care.

—*Thea Cannon.*


## WIND TRICKS
*Beginners and Primary*

The wind is full of tricks today—
He blew my daddy's hat away.
>(Pretend to sweep hat off head.)

He chased our paper down the street.
>(Chase fluttering left hand with right hand.)

He gives scraps either wings or feet.
>(Use hands for "wings" and two fingers for "feet.")

He makes the trees and bushes dance.
>(With arms raised, make dancing motions with arms and body.)

Just listen to him howl and prance!
>(Listen and waggle a pointed finger.)

—*Thea Cannon.*

19

# HELPERS

# TEN LITTLE CHILDREN

*Primary*

Once there were ten little children
(That's really quite a few.)
They did so many, many things
That children like to do.

(Left hand.)
This little girl washed the dishes,
This little girl swept the floor,
This little girl helped her mother
With many an odd little chore.
This little girl loved her daddy
And all the rest of them, too,
And this little tiny baby
Was ready to laugh and coo.

(Right hand.)
This little boy brought the water,
This little boy brought the wood,
This little boy helped his father
To do all the things that he could.
This little boy rocked the cradle
And sang little brother a song.
Indeed, they were all very happy,
Being helpful all the day long.

(Let the children act out the poem, stretching themselves all
over as they do so, thus resting the big muscles. Let them
stretch up, as if hanging clothes on a line, for "This little
girl helped her mother with many an odd little chore."
The action for "This little girl loved her daddy, and all the
rest of them, too," should be hugging themselves tightly,
and for "And this little tiny baby was ready to laugh and
coo," should be as if rocking a baby in their arms. Other
actions are self-explanatory.)

—*I. Mae Wiles.*

# WHEN I GROW UP

*Primary*

When I grow up big and tall,
(Stand on tiptoes and stretch arms up high.)
A good helper I will be.
A helper to father
(Thumb.)
Who is kind and good.
I'll do for my mother
(First finger.)
The things I should.
A helper to sister,
(Second finger.)
To brother, too;
(Third finger.)
A helper to all
My friends so true.
(Fourth finger.)
And God's helper I'll try to be,
By loving others as He loves me.
(Hands folded as in prayer.)
I want to be a helper of all,
(Wide sweep of arms.)
When I grow up big and tall.
(Stand on tiptoes and stretch arms up high.)

—*Selected.*

# THE HELPERS

*Primary*

Two little eyes to see nice things to do,
(First fingers put lightly on eyes.)
Two little lips to smile the whole day through,
(First fingers lightly on lips.)
Two little ears to hear what others say,
(First fingers lightly on ears.)
Two little hands to put our toys aways,
(Hands extended in front, open and palms up.)
A tongue to speak sweet words each day,
(First finger on tongue.)
A loving heart for work or play,
(Both hands over heart.)
Two feet that errands gladly run,
(Bend slightly and first fingers point to feet.)
Make happy days for every one.

—*Louise M. Oglevee.*

# THE DOCTOR
*Primary*

I'd like to be a doctor,
> (Point to self with pride.)

And help some one who's sick.

My case I'd open quickly,
> (Open imaginary case.)

And first take out a stick.
> (Pull out and hold up stick.)

I'd look down the throat carefully,
> (Hold head firm with left hand, and manipulate stick with right.)

And never cause a tear.
> (Shake head negatively.)

Then with a light I'd take a peek
> (Pretend to hold light and peek in ears.)

Into each little ear.

Next with a stethescope I'd hear
> (Place imaginary stethescope over ears and pretend to listen to chest of patient.)

Just what went on inside.

"A little pill, a day in bed,
> (While saying last two lines, give out pill and close case.)

Is just what I prescribe."

—*Thea Cannon.*

## THE MILKMAN
*Beginners and Primary*

I drive my truck along the street,
  (Steer imaginary truck.)

Then at a house I stop.
  (With left hand pull up the brake.)

I take the bottles carefully
  (Put bottles carefully in imaginary wire basket for this line and next.)

So not a one I drop.

Then rattle, rattle to the door—
  (Carry heavy rack with bottles.)

I leave the milk, and then
  (Leave milk and pick up empty bottles.)

With "empties" I go to my truck
  (Swing light rack with empty bottles.)

And drive along again.
  (Steer, as in first line.)

—*Thea Cannon.*

# ONE LITTLE HELPER

*Beginners*

This little girl does nothing but play;
This little one *will* have her way;
This is a girl so strong and tall;
This bad child will not help at all.
Here's one who's kind and true,
Always helping—just like you.

(Fingers of left hand are held up. Child points to each
finger in turn with forefinger of right hand. Substitute
"boy" or "girl" when desired.)

—*Unknown.*

# THE CARPENTER

*Nursery or Beginners*

The carpenter's hammer goes rap, rap, rap,
And his saw goes see, saw, see;
He planes and measures and hammers and saws
While he builds a house for me.

(The doubled-up hand makes the hammer; the open hand,
slanting downward and moved back and forth as in sawing,
makes the saw; the right hand, with fingers closed, is moved
back and forth for the plane, and the measuring is indicated
by both hands as if using a long tape or ruler. The arms and
hands over the head may make the pointed roof of the
finished house.)

—*Louise M. Oglevee.*

# THE BUSY FINGERS

*Nursery or Beginners*

Little busy finger people,
Who will put the toys away?
"I will," "I will," "I will," "I will,"
"I will," all the fingers say.

(The busy fingers may be asked to do many things. Perhaps
it may be, "Who will hang this up today?" as they are helped
to hang up caps and coats. Or, "Who will help us work
today?" when there is work to be done. At each "I will"
the fingers, which have been lighty doubled up, come out and
are held up—first the thumbs, then the index fingers,
and so on. As a rest exercise the verse may say, "Who will
help us play today?" or "Who will help us clap today?"
or "Who will help us wave today?")

—*Louise M. Oglevee.*

# THE ENGINEER
*Beginners*

I ride in the engine,
> (Point to self proudly.)

The whistle I blow.
> (Pull imaginary whistle cord.)

I do all the things that will make the train go.
> (Use imagination—pull out throttle, etc.)

"Whoo! Whoo!" says the whistle!
> (Put hands to mouth, and draw out "whoo whoo.")

"Chug! Chug!" say the wheels!
> (Use arms as wheel motions.)

I'm chief engineer till I'm called for my meals.
> (Pat chest proudly.)

*—Thea Cannon.*


# THE DIGGER
*Beginners and Primary*

I'm a digger, big and strong—
> (Puff out chest and pat with both hands.)

Here's my arm; it's very long.
> (Extend left arm stiff and pat with right hand to show "long."

Here's my hand, and with a spurt
> (Wiggle fingers of left hand, arm still extended stiffly; at "spurt," drop extended arm to floor and scoop up dirt; then back to previous position.)

I clutch the ground and bring up dirt.
I turn and drop it in the truck;
> (Turn whole trunk, left arm still extended, and open fist to drop "dirt.")

Then start all over—chuck! chuck! chuck!
> (Again bring hand to floor.)

*—Thea Cannon.*

# THE PEDAL POEM
*Beginners and Primary*

My tricycle is a trusty friend;
    (Hold hand out toward imaginary tricycle.)

I push and pedal without end.
    (Hands on pedals in bicycle motion.)

Sometimes fast and sometimes slow,
    (Pedal fast, then slow.)

On many errands we can go.
    (Spread out all ten fingers for many.)

For mother or a friend next door
    (Fling out one hand for "mother," other for "friend.")

I pedal to the grocery store.
    (Pedal motion with hands.)

Sometimes I pedal, just for fun,
    (Continue pedal motion.)

Faster than a child can run.
    (Pedal with hands as fast as possible.)

—*Thea Cannon.*

# MISSIONARY

# IN AFRICA
*Primary*

I'd like to go to Africa
>(Point to self.)

Where natives build straw huts like this;
>(Join fingertips of two hands and form thatched roof.)

Where elephants have big, gray trunks;
>(Use both arms with hands clasped, and swing trunk in front of you.)

Where native arrows seldom miss;
>(Shoot arrow in pantomime.)

Where lions shake their manes and roar;
>(Shake head and roar with word "roar.")

Where everything's a little odd.
I'd like to go to Africa
>(Point to self.)

And teach about the one true God.
>(Fling arms wide.)

*—Thea Cannon.*

# THE WORLD CHILDREN

*Beginners and Primary*

This is a Chinese,
(Point to thumb of left hand.)
His skin is yellow.
This is an African,
(Point to index finger.)
Such a nice little fellow!
This is an Eskimo,
(Point to middle finger.)
Round and fat.
This is a Mexican
(Point to third finger.)
With a great big hat.
This little fellow is very fine,
(Point to little finger.)
He has a face that looks like mine.
Jesus loves all of us, you see,
(Hold up all fingers.)
And we will try like Him to be.

—*Selected.*

# PLAYING TOGETHER

*Primary*

Four little boys sat on a bus,
(Left hand into a fist [bus]; place right hand on back of left
with fingers pointing up, but they are bent down.)
One named Tony and one named Gus,
(Hold up a finger for each child.)
One named Woo and one named Pete,
(Hold up fingers; now four are up; thumb is still down.)
Along came Hulda and wanted a seat.
(Now pop up the thumb.)
Five little children as different as could be,
(Hold up right hand.)
Yet they are happy, like you and me.
(Wiggle fingers.)
Five little children get off the bus,
(Walk fingers across lap.)
Their names were Woo, Tony, Hulda, Pete, and Gus.
(Hold up fingers one at a time in rapid order starting with
the thumb.)

—*Hazel Kitchell Evans.*

# JESUS' LOVE

*Nursery and Beginners*

Jesus loves all children—
The ones still very small,
> (Use hand to indicate knee-high child.)

The baby in the cradle,
> (Form cradle with arms and rock.)

The ones so big and tall.
> (Hands high over head.)

—*Thea Cannon.*

# TRAVELING

*Nursery and Beginners*

When I am big I'll travel far,
> (Point to self, then fling arms wide.)

Where Eskimos and igloos are.
> (Turn and point finger "far off.")

I'll go by boat or fly by air,
> (Paddle motion, then flying plane with crossed hands in air.)

And teach about God everywhere.
> (Bring hands to chest in folded position, then fling arms wide.)

—*Thea Cannon.*

# TURN ABOUT

*Primary*

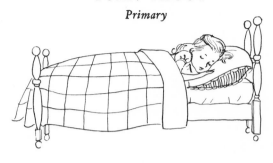

When the sun is shining bright,
> (Left hand high for sun.)

And I am hard at play,
> (Emphasize "I" and point to self or imitate some "play.")

The little Chinese boys and girls
> (Emphasize "Chinese" and point to distance.)

Are dreaming far away.
> (Assume sleep pose.)

But when the stars are shining bright,
> (Use fingers for winking stars.)

And I'm tucked in my bed,
> (Sleep pose.)

The Chinese children fly their kites,
> (Fly imaginary kite.)

With sunshine overhead.

—*Thea Cannon.*

# Bible Stories

# SHARING
## Primary

When Jesus asked for food to share,
A very little boy
(Hold out hand to indicate small boy.)

Brought forth his fish and loaves of bread
(Use hands to show size of fish and size of loaf; loaf slightly larger.)

And saw, with utmost joy,
(Clap once to show joy.)

How Jesus gave to every one.
(Pretend to hand out food to many.)

Thousands were well fed,
(Make huge arc with hands and arms as if denoting a large multitude.)

Because one very little boy
(Repeat first motion.)

Shared his fish and bread.
(Repeat second motion.)

—*Thea Cannon.*

## BABY MOSES

Here in your basket-boat, sleep baby dear,
Bye-lo, Bye-lo.
Sister is watching and always is near,
Bye-lo, Bye-lo.

> (The cupped hands together make the basket, the thumbs
> together, down inside, for the baby. The boat gently rocks
> back and forth as you say the verses.)

—*Unknown.*

## THE CLOCK

*Nursery and Beginners*

"Ticktock, ticktock,
Ticktock," says the clock;
"Little boy, little girl,
Time for Bible school."

> (The whole arm may swing like the pendulum of the big
> clock, and the hand from the wrist may be the little clock.
> The clock may tell the children to do many things, thus
> making play of a task; such as, for the last line, "Put the
> blocks away" or "Time to tell the story" or "Time to wash
> your hands.")

—*Louise M. Oglevee.*

## THE GREAT ARK BOAT

*Nursery and Beginners*

The great ark boat goes sailing by,
But the people inside are safe and dry,
And animals big, and animals small,
Are not afraid in the ark at all.

When the rain stops, big doors open wide,
And people and animals come outside.
Then, oh, how happy they all will be
The bright warm sunshine again to see!

> (Put the doubled fists together, with thumbs upright for the
> door. The touching knuckles make the ridge of the roof.
> Move back and forth as if floating on the water. "When the
> rain stops," put fists on the table, backs up, and when the
> thumb doors are raised, let the finger people and animals
> come out one by one.)

—*Louise M. Oglevee.*

35

## BRAVE DANIEL
### Primary

Brave Daniel in the lions' den
(Use voice to indicate bravery.)
Didn't think of fear.
(Shake head negatively.)
He bowed his head and prayed to God
(Fold hands and bow head in prayer.)
With all the lions near.
(Make arc with hands and arms to show lions all around.)
Next morning when the sun came up,
(Point toward sky.)
The king called, "Are you there?"
(Cup hand by mouth and lower head.)
"Oh, yes!" Brave Daniel called to him,
(Cup hand and raise head.)
"God kept me in His care!"

—*Thea Cannon.*

# BUILDING
*Beginners*

When Jesus was a little boy,
   (Hold out hand to indicate little.)

His saw and hammer were a joy.
   (Saw is one hand sawing on other, and hammer is pounding one fist on other.)

I like to build.  It's fun, I've found,
   (Point to self.)

To saw, saw, saw, and pound, pound, pound!
   (Sawing and hammering motions.)

—*Thea Cannon.*


# THE SHEPHERD BOY
*Beginners and Primary*

David liked to tend his sheep.
   (Assume shepherd pose, holding staff and putting hand to forehead as if watching flock.)

He'd rest against a tree or rock;
   (Lean back as if against tree or rock in restful pose.)

He'd play his harp and make up songs,
   (Strum imaginary harp held in left hand.)

And stop to pet his woolly flock.
   (Pretend to pet sheep.)

—*Thea Cannon.*

# Special Days

## OUR TURKEY

*Beginners and Primary*

Our turkey is a big fat bird
> (Spread arms and hands in a big circle in front of you.)

Who gobbles when he talks.
His red chin's always drooping down;
> (Dangle both hands under chin, the fingers of one touching the wrist of the other.)

He waddles when he walks.
> (Hands on hips and shift weight from one foot to the other for "waddle.")

His tail is like a spreading fan,
> (Link thumbs together and spread fingers wide for large fan.)

And on Thanksgiving Day,
> (Hold same position.)

He sticks his tail high in the air
> (Keep same position and move "fan" high over head.)

And *whoosh* he flies away!
> (Unlock thumbs and bring arms in wide, fast arc to sides.)

*—Thea Cannon.*

## ON MOTHER'S DAY
### Beginners and Primary

I have a mother, kind and sweet.
> (Point to self.)

She dusts and keeps our house so neat;
> (Make dusting, sweeping motions, or any others children think of.)

She washes dishes, irons our clothes.
> (Let child make up dish-washing or ironing motion—or help.)

When I need help she always knows
> (Place hands on chest for "I" and hold palms up in front for "always.")

Exactly what is good and right.
> (Waggle index finger for "exactly," "good," and "right.")

For her—a special prayer tonight.
> (Fold hands in prayer.)

—*Thea Cannon.*

# ON FATHER'S DAY

*Beginners and Primary*

I have a Daddy, big and strong,
(Throw back shoulders and pat chest.)

Who works for us the whole day long.
(Imitate father's work.)

He always knows a game that's fun;
(Imitate any game played with Dad.)

He reads to us when day is done.
(Use hands to make open. book.)

I'd like to bow my head and pray:
(Bow head and fold hands.)

God bless my daddy *every* day.

—*Thea Cannon.*

41

# GEORGE WASHINGTON

*Primary*

Before George Washington was great,
He was a little child like me.
(Point to self.)
He even did some naughty things,
(Waggle pointed index finger.)
Like chopping down a cherry tree.
(Grasp imaginary hatchet and chop.)
He told his father what he'd done,
Because he never told a lie.
(Shake head negatively.)
I'll try, when I do naughty things,
(Bow head and point to self.)
To say, "Dear Father, it was I."

—*Thea Cannon.*


# TWINKLE STARS

*Nursery and Beginners*

Twinkle, twinkle, twinkle, twinkle,
Stars of Christmas Day.
"Merry Christmas! Merry Christmas!"
This is what they say.
(Fingers on upraised hands are the Christmas stars.)

—*Louise M. Oglevee.*


# FOURTH OF JULY

*Beginners and Primary*

Today's the Fourth. My horn I toot;
(Hold imaginary horn to mouth.)
I beat my drum while fireworks shoot.
(Beat "drum" with both hands.)
I watch the flares shoot up so high,
(Bring both hands high over head quickly, and stand on
tiptoes.)
And burst like flowers in the sky.
(Bring hands back to side in wide circle.)

—*Thea Cannon.*

# AN EASTER STORY
*Primary*

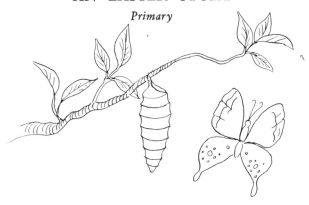

A fuzzy, orange caterpillar
> (Inch index finger of right hand over left hand and out on a finger for the next line.)

Climbed out upon a twig,
Where he soon spun a gray cocoon
> (Hands together with finger-tips touching and knuckles slightly out for cocoon effect.)

That wasn't very big.
> (Use index fingers to show length.)

There he stayed all snug and warm
> (Cross arms with hands on shoulders in hugging-self attitude.)

Until one sunny day—
> (Clap hands once in surprise.)

The gray cocoon just opened up,
> (Start with hands in cocoon shape and slowly unfold.)

And there, so bright and gay,
A butterfly with orange wings
> (Hands together at wrists, using hands for butterfly wings.)

Flew merrily away.
> (As above and flap "wings" in flight.)

*—Thea Cannon.*

# IN THE STABLE
## *Primary*

Where cattle and donkeys and woolly sheep lay,
>(Put out hand to indicate imaginary animal's location.)

The sweet baby Jesus was born Christmas Day.
>(Sleep pose with head on hands.)

The shepherds and Wise-men from near and from far
>(Shepherds hold imaginary staff, and Wise-men assume thinking pose with finger on chin. Show "near" and "far" with alternate hands.)

Had seen the bright light or the wondrous star.
With gifts that were precious, and worshiping hearts,
>(Hold palms up as presenting gifts; hand over heart.)

They traveled by foot or by camels or carts.
>(Imitate modes of travel.)

They knelt by the Baby, their heads bowed in prayer,
>(Kneel and fold hands.)

While Mary rocked Jesus with tend'rest care.
>(Rock "Baby" in arms.)

*—Thea Cannon.*

# A CHRISTMAS-TREE STORY

*Primary*

Down deep in the forest where trees grow so tall,
> (Hands high over head.)

Stood one little fellow, the smallest of all!
> (Arm out to indicate knee-high tree. Use this for each "smallest of all" in whole poem.)

The trees waved their branches and rustled their leaves,
> (Wave arms for branches, then shake hands for leaves.)

But the smallest of all just stood stiff in the breeze.
> (Hold arms stiff a little away from body for a Christmas-tree shape.)

When winter winds howled the tall trees were afraid,
> (Raise hands over head and shake as if in fear.)

And dropped all their leaves till there was no more shade.
> (Use fluttering fingers for leaves—start overhead and weave down to ground.)

The smallest of all just stood brave and grew tall,
> (Start with stiff Christmas-tree pose, then raise arm overhead for "grew tall.")

And kept his green coat when snow started to fall.
> (Fluttering finger motion again.)

One day laughing children came pulling a sleigh.
> (Put hands together at one side, and pull "sleigh" to front.)

They laid him on gently and pulled him away.
> (Hands together [palms] and lay sideways as if on sleigh.)

They dressed him in tinsel and bright, shiny balls,
> (Pretend to trim tree in front of you.)

In peppermint canes, tiny angels, and dolls.
> (Trace cane shape with index fingers, then use fingers parallel to indicate size of angels.)

And on Christmas morning 'twas easy to see—
> (Clap hands once, and hold palms together below chin.)

The smallest of all was the loveliest tree.
> (Knee-high motion again, and clap hands once more.)

—*Thea Cannon.*

45

# LITTLE CHRISTMAS TREE
*Beginners and Primary*

I am a little Christmas tree,
(Hands outstretched.)
I'm standing by the door,
(Stand up very straight.)
And I'm so full of presents
I can't hold any more.
(Shake heads.)
Here's a ball for Tommy,
(Hands together to form circle.)
A doll for Susan Lee,
(Rock imaginary doll in arms.)
Billy has some carpenter tools,
(Hammering motion.)
There's a sewing set for Marie.
(Sewing motion.)
I'm just a little Christmas tree,
(Hands outstretched.)
Up here there is a star,
(Put hands on head.)
I have many good gifts, too,
Like the Wise-men from afar.
(Hand to forehead as if looking into the distance.)

*—Selected.*

# THE CHURCH BELL
*Nursery and Beginners*

"Come, come, come, come,"
Listen to the church bells ringing;
"Come, come, you're welcome,"
This is what they say.
(The hands imitate the ringing of the church bells, reaching up and pulling on an imaginary rope. A shorter verse for nursery children is:)

"Come, come," the church bells say,
"Come to church this happy day."
(A special day may be recognized by making the verse say "this Easter Day," or "this Christmas Day," or "this Rally Day.")

*—Louise M. Oglevee.*

# ANIMALS AND BIRDS

# MISS MUFFET'S SPIDER
*Beginners and Primary*

A spider, one fine summer day,
> (Hold left hand up with fingers as spider's legs.)

Made Miss Muffet run away.
> (Bring left hand toward right hand which runs away on two fingers.)

But I sit down to watch him spin
> (Put right fist in front of you, and lift left hand to make spider spin a web.)

A lacy web with thread so thin.
I wonder if Miss Muffet knew
> (Place hands and arms in a thinking pose and hold for last line.)

That God made little spiders, too?

—*Thea Cannon.*


# EACH IN ITS OWN PLACE
*Beginners and Primary*

Pussy's whiskers,
> (Make whiskers at mouth with all ten fingers.)

Rooster's comb,
> (Use one hand with fingers; spread over front part of head.)

Bunny's ears,
> (Use index finger of each hand or hand with fingers together.)

The snail's shell home—
> (Extend two fingers of right hand and cup left hand over right for the house.)

God knows where all of them belong
And never, *never* gets them wrong!

—*Thea Cannon.*

48

# FIVE LITTLE SQUIRRELS

*Beginners and Primary*

Five little squirrels fat,
Frisking around one day.
Soon only four were left,
For one ran away.
(Hold up left hand. Bend thumb in palm of hand.)

Four little squirrels fat,
Playing in a tree.
One scampered off again,
Then there were three.
(Cover with index finger.)

Three little squirrels fat,
Didn't know what to do.
Mother Squirrel called one,
Then there were two.
(Cover with middle finger.)

Two little squirrels fat,
Having lots of fun.
One went and hid himself,
Then there was one.
(Cover with ring finger.)

One little squirrel fat,
Didn't know what to do,
Couldn't play all by himself,
So he ran home, too.
(Bend little finger over, making a closed fist.)

—*Emma F. Bush.*

# FIVE LITTLE SHEEP

*Nursery and Beginners*

This little sheep said, "I just love to eat,"
This little sheep said, "This grass is so sweet,"
This little sheep said, "Some salt for me,"
This little sheep slept under a tree,
This little sheep was out in the dark and cold,
But the shepherd brought him safely back to the fold.
(Begin with thumb of left hand, point with index finger
of right hand to each finger in turn.)

—*Emma F. Bush.*

# FIVE LITTLE KITTENS
*Nursery and Beginners*

There were five little kittens.
One little kitten went to sleep,
Two little kittens went to sleep,
Three little kittens went to sleep,
Four little kittens went to sleep,
Five little kittens went to sleep.
All the kittens were fast asleep.
(Hold left hand up; with right hand fold the left hand
fingers into the palm, one by one, starting with little finger.)

—*Unknown.*

# FIVE LITTLE BIRDS
*Beginners and Primary*

Five hungry little birds eating near the door,
One flew away, and then there were four.
Four hungry little birds down from the tree,
One flew away, and then there were three.
Three hungry little birds twitter "thank you";
One flew away and then there were two.
Two hungry little birds eating in the sun,
One flew away, and then there was one.
One hungry little bird, when crumbs were gone,
Spread his wings and flew away—then there were none.
Five busy little birds all flew away,
But they'll fly back again, this very day.
(Five outspread fingers become the five hungry birds pick-
ing up crumbs. Double up the thumb for the first bird to
"fly away." Then the others double up one by one until all
are gone. Use the right hand, only.) —*Louise M. Oglevee.*

# FIVE LITTLE FROGGIES
*Nursery and Beginners*

This little froggy broke his toe—
This little froggy cried, "Oh, oh, oh!"
(Great deal of expression.)
This little froggy laughed and was glad;
This little froggy cried and was sad;
This little froggy, kind and good,
Hopped after the doctor as fast as he could.
(Little finger to hop away.)

—*Unknown.*

# THIS IS THE WHITE SHEEP
*Nursery and Beginners*

This is the white sheep,
And this is the way
The farmer cut off the wool one day.
The wool was spun
Into thread so fine,
And made into cloth for this coat of mine.

(The left hand is the sheep and the right hand the shears.
Index and middle fingers make the blades that open and close,
and the thumb and other fingers doubled up make the handle.
Instead of "coat" it may be "dress" or "sweater" or any wool
garment that the children are wearing that day.

—*Louise M. Oglevee.*

## LITTLE LAMBS
*Beginners*

Little white lambs come out to play

(Move the fingers about quickly as if they are little lambs
at play.)

In a grassy field on a summer day.

(Stretch arms out to make the grassy meadow.)

They nibble the grass and jump and run,

(Play they nibble the grass by moving the curved fingers up
and down slowly. Then make them jump and run and
scamper away.)

And sleep by their mother when day is done.
Little white lambs are fast asleep,
Beside the dear old mother sheep.

(Interlock the fingers and put them down inside palms turned
together and thumbs under for the mother sheep.)

—*Emilie Poulsson.*

## THE BUSY SQUIRREL
*Nursery*

A little squirrel with a bushy tail
Goes frisking all around,
And ev'ry day he stores away
The nuts that he has found.

(Left arm makes tree, and hand shapes hole for the nuts;
right hand is the squirrel, index and middle fingers running
up the left arm and poking imaginary nuts in the hole.)

—*Louise M. Oglevee.*

# Fall and Winter

# THE NUTS
*Primary*

"Tap, tap, tap," say the nuts, as they fall from the trees
That are swaying and bending about in the breeze.
"We are food for the children and squirrels," they say,
"And we'll help in the feast on Thanksgiving Day."

(The children's bodies are the trees, and their arms the
swaying branches. The fingers imitate the tapping nuts
that all falling upon the ground.) —*Louise M. Oglevee.*

# THE CELLAR
*Beginners and Primary*

Downstairs to the cellar, come let us all go,
Where fruit jars like this we shall see in a row;
Potatoes like this are heaped up in a bin
Near the pumpkins so fat, and the celery thin.

Cabbages big as your head we shall see,
And rosy red apples just picked from the tree.
We'll not fear cold winter, but thankful we'll be
For all of the good things from field, vine, and tree.

(Motions suggest themselves; upright hands and fingers, the
fruit jars; potatoes, hands with finger tips touching; cabbages
and pumpkins, widespread hands with curving fingers. Apples, pears, and grapes are picked from imaginary trees and
vines.) —*Louise M. Oglevee.*

# LITTLE SNOWFLAKES
*Primary*

Merry little snowflakes falling through the air,
Resting on the steeples and tall trees everywhere;
Covering roofs and fences, capping every post,
Covering the hillside where we like to coast.
Merry little snowflakes try their very best
To make a soft, white cover, so buds and flowers may rest.
When the bright spring sunshine says he's come to stay,
Then those merry snowflakes quickly run away!

(The action to this verse may be simple also. Several places
in the room may be "tall trees," "fences," "hillsides," and
so on. Some of the children may be "flowers," some "snowflakes," and one may be the "sunshine." The snowflakes
skip around the room, and with a fluttering motion "cover"
the trees, hillsides, and so on. They "cover" the flowers who
are asleep. Then the sun comes and the snowflakes run away.)

—*Maud Burnham.*

# OUR SNOWMAN
*Primary*

Our snowman has a big, fat tummy,

(Arms and hands out front to form circle.)

And a head that's somewhat smaller.

(Use hands to show size of head.)

The black top hat we have him wear

(Hands on head.)

Makes him seem a little taller.

(Hands and arms over head.)

His carrot nose and coal-black eyes

(Finger to nose, then point to eyes.)

Make him jolly and quite sunny.

The buttons marching down his front,

(Use finger and poke buttons down the front.)

And stony grin are very funny.

(Pull corners of mouth to make grin.)

—*Thea Cannon.*

# SLED RIDING
*Beginners and Primary*

I button up good, and I pull on a glove.

(Make buttoning motions at throat and pull on a "glove.")

I sit on my sled, and I give it a shove.

(Place left hand [you] on back of right hand [sled]; "shove" this sled in a wide arc.)

The snow stings my face and the wind whistles shrill,

(Cover face with both hands for first half; then cover ears.)

As I'm on my sled, flying *zip* down the hill!

(Repeat second motion all the way to floor.)

—*Thea Cannon.*

# SLEEPY MISS CLOVER

*Beginners or Primary*

Little Miss Clover is nodding her head,
Sleepy and tired and all ready for bed.

Kind Mrs. Oak Tree sends fluttering down
A soft, warm blanket of leaves, red and brown.

Rain tucks them in while the autumn winds sing,
And little Miss Clover will sleep till next spring.

(This may be dramatized by the children, one representing
Miss Clover, another the tree, and another the rain, while
two or three at one side sing softly in imitation of the wind.
If preferred, this may be used as a finger-play.)

*—Unknown.*

# SLEEPING FLOWERS

*Nursery and Beginners*

This is the way the flowers sleep,
Under the soft white snow;
This is the way when springtime comes,
Flowers wake and grow.

(Fingers curled under and held in the lap are sleeping flowers.
Fingers together, as closed flower buds, come up slowly,
slowly, higher, higher, and open out as flowers.)

*—Louise M. Oglevee.*

# THE SQUIRREL

*Beginners or Primary*

These are the brown leaves fluttering down,
And this is the tall tree, bare and brown;
This is the squirrel with eyes so bright,
Hunting for nuts with all his might.
This is the hole where, day by day,
Nut after nut he stores away.
When winter comes with cold and storm,
He'll sleep curled up all snug and warm.

(Imitate leaves with both hands; tall tree, left hand, with
fingers outspread; right hand, the squirrel running here and
there; hole, thumb and finger of left hand; right hand curled
up for sleeping squirrel in the branches of the tree.)

*—Louise M. Oglevee.*

# MISCELLANEOUS

# FINGER FAMILY

*Beginners and Primary*

"Good morning, Mother Finger,
(Point to thumb of left hand.)
What will you do today?"
"I'll love you and take care of you,
That's what I'll do today."

"Good morning, Father Finger,
(Point to index finger.)
What will you do today?"
"I'll work hard all day long for you,
That's what I'll do today."

"Good morning, Brother Finger,
(Point to middle finger.)
What will you do today?"
"I'll work and play and help all day,
That's what I'll do today."

"Good morning, Sister Finger,
(Point to ring finger.)
What will you do today?"
"I'll help all day and work and play,
That's what I'll do today."

"Good morning, Baby Finger,
(Point to little finger.)
What will you do today?"
He'll laugh and play and sleep all day,
That's what he'll do today.

—*Louise M. Oglevee.*

# FIVE CHILDREN

*Nursery or Beginners*

Here are five children:
This one swept the floor;
This one went to the store;
This one closed the door;
This, a smile always wore;
This one loved me more.
(Right hand covering each finger of left hand.)

—*Unknown.*

# LITTLE HANDS

*Nursery, Beginners, and Primary*

Open, shut them; open, shut them;
Give a little clap;
Open, shut them; open, shut them;
Lay them in your lap.

Creep them, creep them slowly upward
To the rosy cheek;
Open wide the shining eyes,
Through the fingers peek. .

Open, shut them; open, shut them;
To the shoulders fly;
Let them like the birdies flutter,
Flutter to the sky.

Falling, falling slowly downward,
Nearly to the ground;
Quickly raise them, all the fingers
Twirling round and round.

Open, shut them; open, shut them;
Give a little clap;
Open, shut them; open, shut them;
Lay them in your lap.

(Do motions as poem suggests.)

—*Unknown.*

# FIVE LITTLE BOYS

*Beginners*

Five little boys from Sunday school
(Hold hand up with fingers apart and stiff.)
Went out for a walk one day.
(Move hand as if walking forward.)
The wind blew so hard
It turned them around,
(Turn hand around.)
And they walked the other way.
(Move hand back slowly.)

—*Unknown.*

# THIS IS THE WAY

*Nursery and Beginners*

This is the way the baby does,
Clap—clap—clap—clap;
  (Clap hands.)
This is the way the baby does,
Peek-a-boo, I see you;
  (Peek-a-boo with hands.)
This is the way the baby does,
Creep—creep—creep—creep;
  (Make fingers "walk.")
This is the way the baby does,
Sleep—sleep—sleep—sleep.
  (Lean cheek against folded hands.)

—*Unknown.*

# IN MY LITTLE GARDEN

*Primary*

In my little garden bed,
Raked so nicely over,
First the tiny seed I sow,
Then with soft earth cover.

Shining down, the great round sun
Smiles upon them often;
Little raindrops, pattering down,
Help the seeds to soften.

Then the little plants awake,
Down their roots go creeping;
Up they lift their little heads
Through the dark earth peeping.

High and higher still they climb,
Through the sunny hours;
Till at last the little buds
Open into flowers.

  (Let the children pretend to be seeds as they crouch down on
  the floor. Select a child to be the sun, some one else to be
  the rain. After these two, walking about among the "seeds,"
  the "seeds" will rise up slowly and stand erect.)

—*Louise M. Oglevee.*

## TOUCH EXERCISE

*Nursery and Beginners*

I'll touch my hair, my lips, my eyes,
I'll sit up straight and then I'll rise;
I'll touch my ears, my nose, my chin,
Then quietly sit down again.

*—A. M. Shumate.*

## MY WINDOWS

*Beginners*

In my house are windows two,
(Point to eyes.)
Shining clear and bright:
I can drop the curtains down,
(Close eyes.)
Shutting out the light.
Open, shut them; open, shut them:
(Open and shut eyes slowly.)
Now 'tis dark, now light;
I can see your windows, too,
Letting in the light.

*—Unknown.*

## GOOD MORNING

*Beginners and Primary*

In the morning when these finger people wake up,
The very first thing that they do
Is to each say, "Good morning, good morning, good
morning,
Good morning, good morning to you."
Now they've all come to Sunday school—Mother and
Father,
Brother, Sister, and Baby, too.
And they each say, "Good morning, good morning, good
morning,
Good morning, good morning to you."

(The "good morning" should be well accented to give the
rhythm, with a nod of the head each time. The fingers of
both hands may "bow" to each other and to every one in
the group.)

*—Louise M. Oglevee.*

# A STORY ABOUT BREAD

*Beginners*

This is the way the mill wheel goes,
Round and round, round and round,
Till all the little grains of wheat
To soft, white flour are ground.

This is the way we make our bread,
White and sweet, white and sweet,
Thanking the Father every day
For this good food we eat.

(In the first verse the hands imitate the motion of the stones
that grind the grain into flour. In the second they make
the motions of kneading bread and of shaping it into a loaf.)

*—Louise M. Oglevee.*

# THE FAMILY

*Nursery and Beginners*

I have a fine family here,
(Hold up hand.)
A family full of good cheer:
A father and mother,
(Point to thumb and index finger.)
A sister and brother,
(Third and fourth fingers.)
A baby, so cunning and dear.
(Little finger.)

*—Frances Weld Danielson.*

# WE THANK THEE

*Beginners*

We thank Thee, God, for sunshine bright,
(Arms up, fingers touching to make sun.)
For birds that sing at morning light,
(Arms outstretched as birds flying.)
For happy children everywhere,
(Clap hands loosely.)
And for our mother's loving care.
(Head bowed, hands folded, in prayer posture.)

*—Unknown.*

# THE CHURCH
*Nursery or Beginners*

This is the church where we're happy together;
Ding, dong, ding, dong, hear the bells ring;
Open the door and peep in at the children.
Listen! listen! hear them all sing.

(The thumbs make the door, and the index fingers the steeple in which the bell hangs as it swings back and forth. When the thumb doors open, the two rows of "children" are seen, and they sing any song which the teacher wishes to fit into the thought of the hour, or which the children may choose.)

—*Louise M. Oglevee.*

# MY BOOK
*Beginners or Primary*

This is my book; it will open wide
To show the pictures that are inside.

This is my ball, so big and round,
To toss in the air or roll on the ground.

Here's my umbrella to keep me dry,
When the raindrops fall from the cloudy sky.

This is my kitty; just hear her purr
When I'm gently stroking her soft, warm fur.

(Hands with the palms together make the book. Finger tips touch and hands cup to make the ball. Upright index finger of one hand, with the other hand flat upon it, makes the umbrella. Left hand is the kitty, which the right hand gently strokes.)

—*Louise M. Oglevee.*

# THE HOME
*Nursery and Beginners*

This is the home where we're happy together;
Open the door and there you can see
Mother and Daddy and Sister and Brother,
Busy and happy and kind as can be.

(Put the two fists together. One hand should be on top of the other, so only one set of fingers is inside. The knuckles are doubled down, fingers make the roof and the people under it, and the upright thumb is the door, which, when "opened," shows the "family" inside the home.)

—*Louise M. Oglevee.*

## GOOD NIGHT

*Nursery, Beginners, and Primary*

When I am sleepy and ready for bed,
(Say line with a yawn; rub eyes.)

I kneel on the floor and I bow down my head.
(Do as line indicates.)

After my prayers, I turn out the light,
(Fold hands first part; pull imaginary light switch.)

I pull up the covers all snug for the night.
(Pull covers up to chin and cross arms with hands hugging shoulders.)

—*Thea Cannon.*